# CHINA
## WORLD ADVENTURES

BY STEFFI CAVELL-CLARKE

KidHaven
PUBLISHING

Published in 2018 by
**KidHaven Publishing, an Imprint of Greenhaven Publishing, LLC**
353 3rd Avenue
Suite 255
New York, NY 10010

© 2018 Booklife Publishing
This edition is published by arrangement with Booklife Publishing.

Designer: Drue Rintoul
Editor: Steffi Cavell-Clarke

**Cataloging-in-Publication Data**

Names: Cavell-Clarke, Steffi.
Title: China / Steffi Cavell-Clarke.
Description: New York : KidHaven Publishing, 2018. | Series: World adventures | Includes glossary and index.
Identifiers: ISBN 9781534524033 (pbk.) | 9781534524026 (library bound) | ISBN 9781534525207 (6 pack) | ISBN 9781534524040 (ebook)
Subjects: LCSH: China–Juvenile literature.
Classification: LCC DS706.C38 2018 | DDC 951–dc23

Printed in the United States of America

CPSIA compliance information: Batch #CW18KL: For further information contact Greenhaven Publishing LLC, New York, New York at 1-844-317-7404.

Please visit our website, www.greenhavenpublishing.com. For a free color catalog of all our high-quality books, call toll free 1-844-317-7404 or fax 1-844-317-7405.

# CHINA
## WORLD ADVENTURES

## CONTENTS

Words in **bold** can be found in the glossary on page 24.

# WHERE IS CHINA?

China is a one of the largest countries in the world. China is between India, Mongolia, and Japan.

MONGOLIA

JAPAN

INDIA

CHINA

# BEIJING

The capital city of China is Beijing.

The **population** of China is more than one billion. China has the highest population in the world.

# WEATHER AND LANDSCAPE

Mount Everest is the highest mountain in the world.

China is very large, so it has lots of different landscapes. It has rivers, mountains, deserts, and forests.

Each of these landscapes has a different **climate**. The mountains are very cold and the deserts are very hot.

AVATAR HALLELUJAH MOUNTAIN

THE GOBI DESERT

# CLOTHING

Many people who live in China wear comfortable and practical clothing. Sometimes, traditional clothing is worn on special occasions.

There are many different types of traditional clothing in China, but mostly, the clothes are made out of silk covered with **embroidery**.

In China, the color red is believed to ward off evil spirits.

**CHEONGSAM**

# RELIGION

China is home to many religions. The religions with the most followers are Confucianism, Taoism, and Buddhism. But everyone in China celebrates Chinese New Year.

Chinese New Year lasts for fifteen days and involves lots of celebrations. Families come together to watch street parades and firework displays.

Dragon dances are performed to scare away evil spirits.

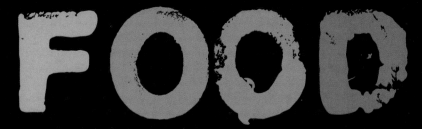

# FOOD

A Chinese meal often has a few small bowls of rice, noodles, and some vegetables. A popular dish in China is a stir-fry.

Chinese food is traditionally eaten with chopsticks. Chopsticks are long, thin wooden sticks. They are held in one hand and used to pick up small pieces of food.

CHOPSTICKS

Children in China start school at the age of six. They study Chinese, English, geography, math, and art.

Every Monday morning, children at primary school raise the Chinese flag and sing the **national anthem**.

The Chinese flag is red with five yellow stars.

# AT HOME

In the cities, many Chinese people live in apartments. There are so many people in China that sometimes more than one family has to share one apartment.

In the small villages, houses are often made out of wood and stone. They have a tiled roof and a small garden called a courtyard.

# FAMILIES

In China, grandparents are treated with respect and kindness. They are often cared for by other members of the family at home.

Families like to get together to celebrate special occasions. They celebrate by eating special food and playing games together.

# SPORTS

Chinese martial arts are traditional sports in China. Martial arts are fighting techniques, which can be used to protect yourself.

**Chinese martial arts are also called kung fu.**

Children in China like to fly kites after school. Chinese kites are bright and colorful.

KITE FLYING IN CHINA

# FUN FACTS

The Great Wall of China was built thousands of years ago. The Great Wall is 13,170 miles long.

It is so long that it can be seen from space.

China is home to the giant panda, the only place where it still lives in the wild.

Pandas love to eat bamboo.

# GLOSSARY

**climate:** the weather in a large area

embroidery: a raised pattern sewn into fabric

**national anthem:** a song that represents a country

population: amount of people living in that place

**traditional:** ways of behaving that have been done for a long time

# INDEX